All My Best

Adventures

Are With You

By

Sean

and

Jackson

Leary

All My Best Adventures Are With You is copyright 2018 Sean Leary. All material in this book is copyright 2018 Sean Leary. All rights reserved, including the right of reproduction in whole or in part in any form including book, audio, video, computer disc, CD-ROM, multimedia, blog, Internet, and all other forms, whether or not yet known or developed.

Material within may not be reprinted or broadcast without the express permission of the author, unless in a promotional capacity. If used in a promotional capacity, all work within must be credited to the author and it must be noted that the work appeared in **All My Best Adventures Are With You**, by Sean and Jackson Leary. This book is published in the United States by Dreaming World Books and distributed worldwide by Amazon / Ingram / Dreaming World Books.

ISBN # (Print book) 978-1-948662-00-0. Library of Congress Catalog Card Number: Applied for

Cover and interior design by Sean and Jackson Leary. Illustrations by Jackson Leary.

Website: www.seanleary.com. Email: seanleary@seanleary.com.

All
My
Best
Adventures
Are
With
You

For Jackson

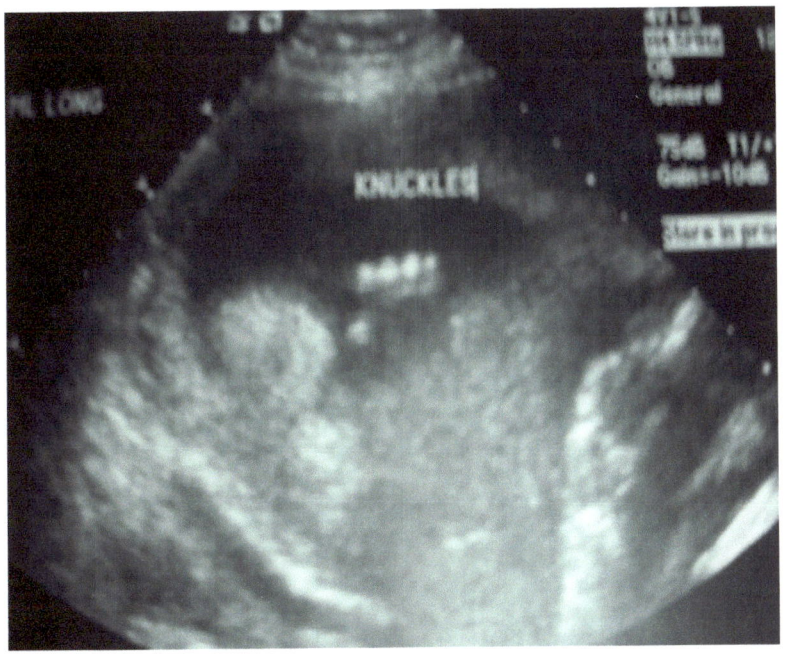

From the first time I saw you

From the first time we met

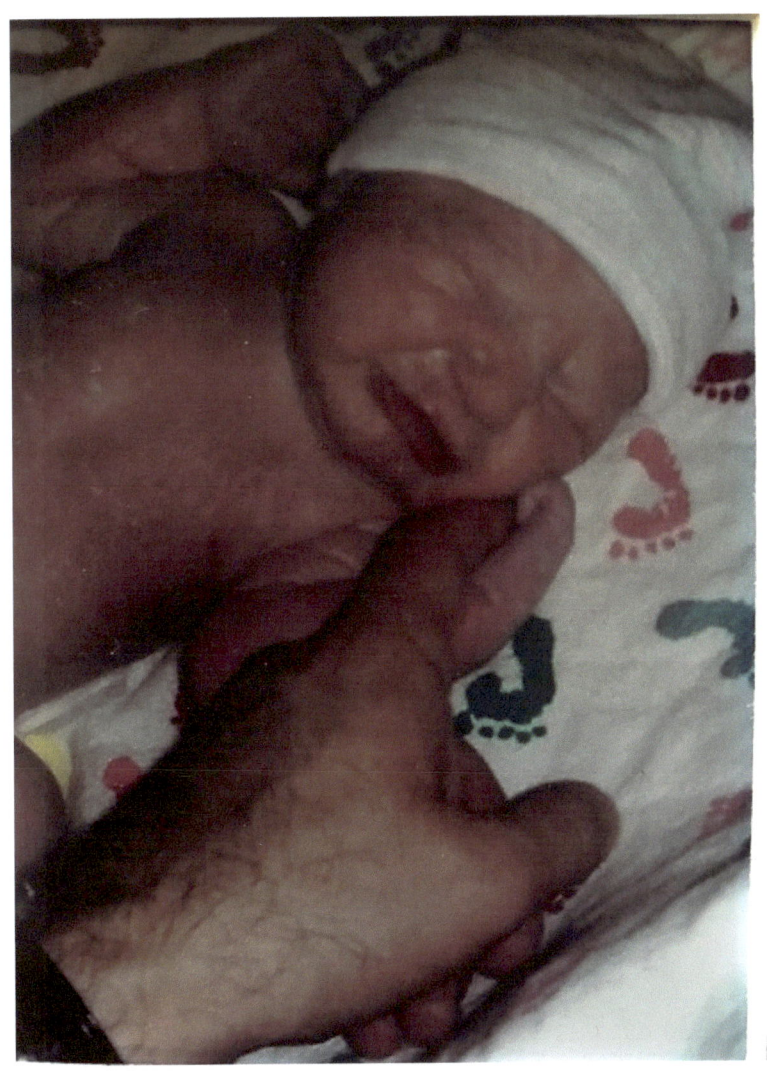

From our first finger hugger

I knew we were going to be best friends.

And I knew

We were going to have so many great adventures together.

And I couldn't wait to have them with you.

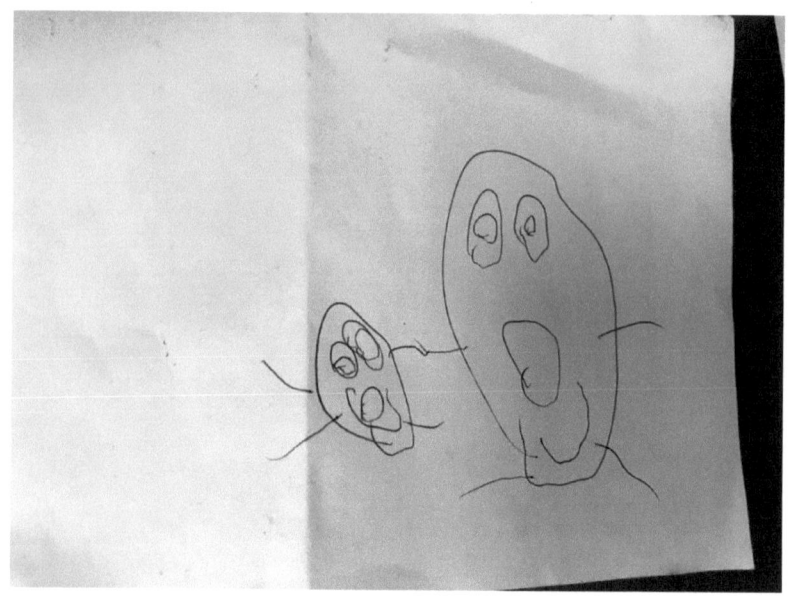

We have had so much fun from the start

Two best friends, the best of friends, who never want to be apart.

We've taken walks

And played hide and seek.

We've gone to movies

And seen theater shows.

We've gone to big concerts

And smaller shows.

We've sung songs

And played at open mic nights.

We've played with cars and trucks

And made snowmen.

We've drawn pictures

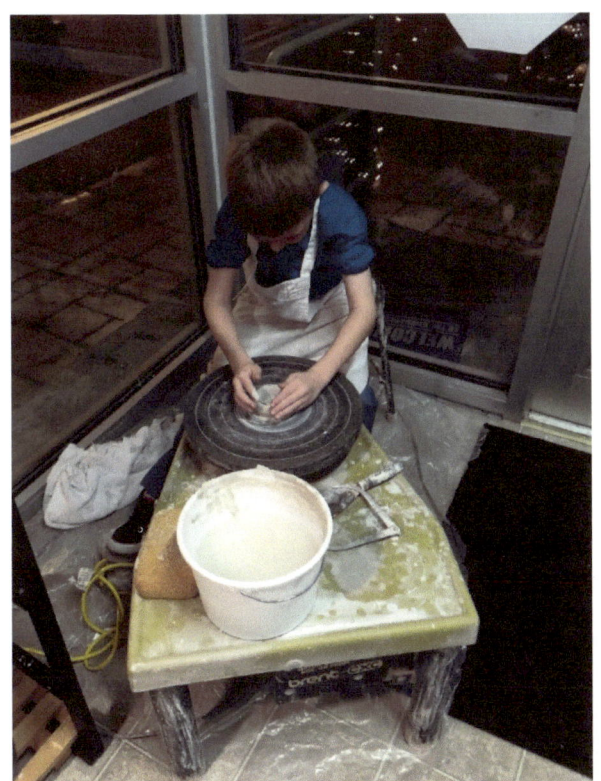

And made pottery

And decorated pumpkins

And cookies

And done lots of other art projects.

And even had our artworks in a gallery!

We've collected pine cones and cool rocks

And made pizzas.

We've played with little engines

And gone to see little engines

And big engines!

And giant claws!

We've met aardvarks...

And penguins...

And Ewoks...

And droids...

And robot rock stars...

And other strange characters!

We've learned it's important to respect all life...

Big and small.

We've played on playgrounds

And had picnics.

We've played drums

And played guitars

And talked to hermit crabs.

We've played baseball

And basketball

And hockey

And other sports.

And paintball...

And nerf battles and video games and chess and cards and board games...

And soccer!

Lots and lots of soccer!

We've read books together

We've spent Halloween together...

And Thanksgiving...

Yummy Thanksgiving...

And Christmas

And New Year's Eve

And all other holidays.

And we've created our own traditions and holidays and special memories along the way.

We've won trophies and celebrated victories...

We've had our Every Saturday traditions...

Had great birthday parties...

Gone to outdoor festivals....

Played outside...

Gone to school programs...

Gone to baseball and soccer games...

And even made books together!

We've done fun, goofy things

Happy to be with this fella again

We've run errands and done chores

And had all sorts of funny adventures.

We have worked and played

We have made new friends

We have learned so many things

And we have grown in so many ways.

We have eaten good foods and tried cool new things...

We have taken care of each other when we've been sick or down or sad...

Encouraged and supported each other

And laughed and smiled together, and always, always, been there for each other.

We've talked and talked and talked... and I've loved listening to you talk about your hopes and dreams and interests.

We have been together through tough days

And easy, relaxed days.

We have gone on field trips...

And road trips, and other journeys…

And stood by each other's side through many things...

And there's nobody else I would've rather been with than you

With your hand holding mine

And your arms always open for huggers.

The best huggers!

And I know

We have so, so, so many more great adventures yet to come...

And I know

I can't wait to experience them with you.

My best friend

My favorite person

Because all my best adventures are with you

And the best adventure

Is life with you.

By my side

And in my heart.

Because from the first time I saw you,

I loved you.

I always have.

And I always will.

And through the journey of life

And all of its adventures

All of its great adventures

I will love you.

Because you're not just my friend,

You're my best friend.

And you always will be.

Always.

Because all my best adventures are with you.

I love you, Jackson.

Thank you for being my son.

And thank you for ten magical, amazing, wonderful years together.

I look forward to many, many, many more years together, and many, many, many more adventures together.

Oh my!

Other Books By Sean Leary

The Arimathean (novel)

The Blood of Destiny (novel)

Black Knight Apocalypse (novel)

The Arimathean Files (non-fiction)

Luna Death Trigger (novel)

DisIntegration (novel)

Does The Shed Skin Know It Was Once A Snake? (short stories)

Every Number Is Lucky To Someone

(short stories)

My Life As A Freak Magnet

(short stories)

Exorcising Ghosts

(graphic novel)

Here Comes The Goot!

(children's/beginning readers)

Go, Racecars, Go!

(children's/beginning readers)

Nine Little Penguin Ninjas

(children's/beginning readers)

Baby Bird

(children's/beginning readers)

We Are All Characters

(children's/beginning readers)

Beautiful Remnants of Chaotic Failures

(poetry)

Danger Maps

(poetry)

Every Broken Heart Creates The Pieces That Will Pave The Way To The Place Your Heart Will Call Home

(poetry)

Tricks of the Light

(poetry)

The Soft Venom of Promise

(poetry)

The Night Universal

(poetry)

There Is Truth In The Untamed Beat of a Heart

(poetry)

We Are Shadows In The Absence of Light

(poetry)

Magnets & Mysteries, Soft Curves & Comets

(poetry)

Infinite Sky

(poetry)

Physics & Beauty

(poetry)

Dark Equinox

(graphic novel)

The Ink In The Well

(graphic novel)

Dream States

(graphic novel)

Valentine Cords

(graphic novel)

Spyder

(graphic novel)

Sean Leary's Greatest Hits, volume one

(humor)

Sean Leary's Greatest Hits, volume two

(humor)

Sean Leary's Greatest Hits, volume three

(humor)

Sean Leary's Greatest Hits, volume four

(humor)

Sean Leary's Greatest Hits, volume five

(humor)

Sean Leary's Greatest Hits, volume six

(humor)

Sean Leary's Greatest Hits, volume seven

(humor)

Your Favorite Band

(stageplay / screenplay)

Dingo Boogaloo

(stageplay / screenplay)

Rock City Live!

(stageplay / screenplay)

My Life As A Freak Magnet: The Scripts

(stageplay / screenplay)

Shots To The Heart, volumes one and two

(stageplays)

Advice to My Son

(life stories and positive parenting)

Do Vampires Poop?

(humor)

The Devil Shops At Target

(humor)

I Don't Have The Map

(poetry)

For more writing and more information, see www.seanleary.com.

I love you, son.

www.ingramcontent.com/pod-product-compliance
Lightning Source LLC
Chambersburg PA
CBHW041625220426
43663CB00001B/16